When Love Hurts:

Healing from the grief caused by infidelity in any relationship

By

Henrietta J. Path

TABLE OF CONTENTS

INTRODUCTION

The fact that extramarital affairs are so prevalent is a source of great regret, but the reality is that they almost always take both parties by surprise. The majority of respondents stated that they had never considered the possibility that either they or their partner could engage in such behavior. It's easy to ignore the signs that there's a hole in our emotional lives, which leaves us open to being exploited. In all honesty, we simply do not comprehend the magnitude of the task that lies ahead of us in protecting and preserving our marriages and other committed relationships.

The primary reason for people having extramarital affairs is because they are searching for love in all the wrong places. When contentment can only come from within, we have a natural urge to reflexively search for it in other places, such as other people or other things. In a strange twist of fate, we are able to attract and establish the ideal romantic relationship only after we have first cultivated the connection that exists within ourselves. In most cases, we gain this knowledge through the school of hard knocks, which explains why I see so many broken couples coming in after it was revealed that one of them had been having an affair. It is the "Wake Up Call" that many people require in order to begin the challenging and exciting process of working on themselves and obtaining an understanding of how to establish love that lasts and deepens over time.

There is cause for optimism for married people who are dealing with infidelity. The most important things are hard work, open and honest communication, patience, and a willingness to improve. When an affair is exposed, it frequently marks the beginning of a crucial period of growth and healing, both for the individuals involved in the relationship as well as for the relationship as a whole. A good number of people emerge from the crisis of infidelity stronger and more dedicated. Even though I don't suggest having an affair, statistics show that the majority of partners can move on after an affair.

When either you or your partner has an affair, it does not automatically mean that you are with the wrong person. Realizing that whatever issues you and your partner face in the relationship, whatever lack or challenge or frustration, these are reflections of where you need to grow in order to be happier, more fulfilled, and the best version of yourself, is the most important and critical key to healing from an affair. We possess a remarkable and innate ability to mend wounds, move on with our lives, and begin a new chapter.

Having said that, a marriage can fail despite the absence of trust, the healing of wounds, and the absence of lies. This is especially true for relationships in which issues have been chipping away at the foundation for a considerable amount of time. Sometimes, it is simply too late, or there is not enough willingness to put in the work necessary to do what needs to be done. Each individual reacts to betrayal in their own unique way.

It is recommended that couples Communicate openly and honestly, be vulnerable with one another, be willing to grow and change, commit to a new and improved relationship, invest in and prioritize the relationship, learn what went wrong, understand their partner, understand themselves; and realize that the pain they are experiencing is a wake-up call to help them become happier and more fulfilled individuals.

CHAPTER 1
How Can Love Cause So Much Pain?

There is no getting around the fact that love may be painful. It doesn't matter how long you were in a relationship or what caused it to end; feeling upset may be difficult and painful, both emotionally and physically. After all, "broken heart" is a metaphor for a reason; it's not simply a metaphor. But is pain a natural part of love? Let's find out!

One of the greatest poets of all time, Alfred Lord Tennyson, once remarked, "It's better to have loved and lost than never to have loved at all." The only way to protect oneself from the pain that comes with love is to steer clear of it altogether (and even this isn't a foolproof strategy).

Being in love involves allowing yourself to be vulnerable, and allowing yourself to be vulnerable brings with it the possibility that you will be wounded, as well as the possibility that the experience will make you stronger. Being in love means letting yourself be vulnerable. As children, we were frequently told that love is the source of unending happiness, warmth, and fulfilment; nevertheless, this is not always the case. There are moments when love might bring about feelings of anxiety and unease. Keep in mind that you are not the only one going through hell because of love. It is possible for it to occur to anyone. When we are overcome with romantic feelings, our bodies release a rush of molecules that stimulate the pleasure region. At first, you may experience euphoria from this, but the withdrawal symptoms can be both emotionally and physically severe.

Increased levels of the hormone cortisol, which are associated with emotions of anxiety, are caused by romantic attachment. This anxiousness can make both your mental and bodily well-being uncomfortable.

The response to the question, "Is pain a natural part of love?" is yes. All's because your mind and your heart are both involved in the experience of love, which is why it hurts so much!

But there are also other reasons why you may feel as like your feelings are getting trampled on when it comes to your relationships.

1. An Air of Skepticism

Even when you are in the company of another person, there are moments when you cannot be confident that you are both aware of the same information. Especially if you don't communicate well with one another or express how you feel very often in your relationship, it is possible that it could rise to feelings such as dread, loneliness, or even jealousy. This kind of emotional upheaval in a relationship can frequently result in physical symptoms such as headaches or even melancholy.

2. The Scoring Is Done On the Body

As was discussed in the preceding paragraph, love is capable of causing physical pain. The first flush of a relationship ending will cause you to quickly experience withdrawal from all of the dopamine, serotonin, and other endorphins that your brain was releasing. This is similar to how you would have a headache from caffeine withdrawal if you decide to cut back on how much coffee you drink. This becomes even more apparent after the termination of a relationship when your natural endorphin production decreases even lower.

3. Expectations That Were Not Met

It is normal to have preconceived notions about what being in a relationship will be like, but what happens when those notions and the reality don't match up? One more reason why love can be so painful is that it has the potential to be disheartening and distressing. It is unfortunate that human beings have a tendency to fixate on what the future might bring rather than focusing on the present. This leads to constant pondering over what might happen in the future, which in turn leads to disappointment when those expectations are not satisfied.

4. The Disappointment of Being Dumped

Who among us has not been told, "it isn't you, it's me," without being fully certain that no, in fact, it truly is you who is the source of the problem? Even when a break-up turns out to be beneficial in the long term or even in the short term, the rejection of a partner can feel like a devastating blow to the ego. It is considerably more difficult when it comes as a surprise or when there is some form of cheating involved. Rejections in dating can wreak havoc on your self-esteem, forcing you to question your own worth and who you are as a person. This might cause you to question your identity. In light of all of this, it should not come as a surprise that love hurts.

5. Results and Implications of Previous Relationships

Even though we want to think that every new relationship is a clean slate, the fact of the matter is that all of us, regardless of whether those prior relationships were romantic or not, bring the baggage of those experiences with us. Untreated trauma of this kind can result in us destroying our own happiness, even while there are instances when this can be a positive thing (for example, a previous negative experience may help us recognize warning signs in the relationships we have now), but there are also times when it can be a negative thing.

How to Stop Alleviating Your Pain by Relying On Love

There is no foolproof method for avoiding all instances of sadness; nonetheless, there are a few things that you can do to decrease the toll that love takes on both your physical and emotional well-being.

1. Work on improving yourself: Therapy is a remedy that is frequently recommended, but the reason for this is because it is effective for the vast majority of people. There is a direct correlation between the amount of baggage you bring into a relationship and the likelihood that it will cause you harm.

2. Exercising: As was said before, the beginning phases of a romantic relationship are associated with increased production of the feel-good chemical endorphin. You can delay the eventual drop-off in dopamine levels by engaging in other activities that release dopamine, the most important of which is exercise. Studies have shown that engaging in consistent physical activity beginning in our 20s and 30s can, in addition to providing chemical benefits, reduce the risk of developing Alzheimer's disease, osteoporosis, and other age-related issues.

3. Get distracted: There's a reason why the proverb "an idle mind is the Devil's workshop" exists. Distract yourself. Keeping yourself occupied means your brain has less time to fixate on things, whether that be thinking about the future or wondering why the end of your most recent relationship came about. Keeping yourself active can help reduce anxiety and depression.

4. Get off social media: Although social media offers many benefits, such as reconnecting with long-lost acquaintances and maintaining contact with distant family members, it also aggravates our worst inclinations. This is especially true when it comes to a relationship that is not going well or has ended. When you stop viewing the feed of your ex and are unable to take in every aspect of their joyful existence without you on social media, it is much simpler to overcome the sensation that you have been unlucky in love.

5. Make the choice to let it go: One of the greatest ways to stop being hurt by love is to just let it go. Making this decision is one of the best methods to stop being wounded by love. This can be accomplished in a number of ways, including severing all contact with your ex-partner, walking away from a conflict, or determining what your limits are and then not crossing them. The first step toward being able to move on from a past relationship is making the conscious decision to weaken its hold on you.

CHAPTER 2
The Psychology of Infidelity

Infidelity can be one of the most painful experiences a person can go through, and it can lead to dramatic repercussions such as depression, domestic violence, broken relationships, divorce, or even homicide in some situations. It is a common occurrence in every part of the world, and it is possible for it to occur even in the healthiest of relationships. The question is, what motivates people to turn their backs on the people they care about and behave dishonestly? Why do people cheat in the first place, and what kind of mental processes are at play when people engage in such dishonest behavior? We will discuss the psychology of cheating, which is interesting whether you are considering cheating yourself, have been cheated on, or are just curious about what causes people to break away from relationships. According to psychologists, people may cheat for a variety of reasons, including the ones listed below.

1. Cheating can be viewed as an outlet for frustration; in fact, cheating is frequently used as an outlet for irritation and problems that have not been resolved inside a

partnership. People who believe that they are not making progress in their relationship with their partner are more likely to want to avoid confrontation and cheat as a strategy to escape the difficulties they are experiencing with their current partner.

2. You or your partner may have the feeling that you are out of control or that there is no hope: A partner may have the feeling that they are out of control or that there is no hope in a relationship but doesn't want to be furious with their partner or cause a scene because of logistical reasons such as children, lifestyle, or financial concerns, etc. They turn to another person in the hopes of finding comfort and security in this way.

3. In addition to serving as a method of retaliation, dishonesty might be interpreted as an attempt to even the score. A person who engages in passive aggression may cheat in order to vent their resentment over their partner's infidelity in a manner that is non-confrontational but nevertheless harmful.

4. A cheater may suffer from extremely low self-esteem and have a narcissistic vision of how things should be seen in the world. Cheating can be an indication of serious problems in a relationship. Some people have a propensity for seeking attention, and once they have

fulfilled their demands and requirements with one person, they may move on to another in order to validate themselves and satisfy their needs. They do not have a balanced sense of their own value, and as a result, they are constantly seeking comfort from others, which causes them to bounce from one person to another.

5. In situations where a person's spouse does not meet their sexual requirements or does not exhibit a desire to have sexual relations with them, cheating may be seen as a last choice for sexual satisfaction. It is possible that they are experiencing something merely physical and that their partner is not providing them with the desired level of enjoyment. Therefore, in order to fulfil the requirements, a cheater may turn to another person who is able to provide them with what they need or want.

6. Some people have issues with power and control, which can manifest as cheating as a means of control. They can be put off by the idea of being subject to an authoritative individual. Therefore, in order to level the playing field and achieve the sensation of having power and control, they cheat. They see cheating as a form of defiance, a method to show people that they can still exert power and control over situations.

7. Cheating could also be due to the circumstances of the game. It's possible that a person is in a perfectly happy relationship, but the fact that they spend a lot of time with attractive individuals makes them more likely to have an affair despite the fact that they're in a good relationship.

CHAPTER 3
The Stages After the Discovery of Infidelity

The first bomb to go off is the revelation of unfaithfulness. The revelation that the relationship is built on lies, dishonesty, and frequent betrayals is the second bomb that is dropped on the couple. An unfaithful partner might be one of the most heartbreaking things for a person to discover about themselves. A person can be left feeling hurt, alone, and bewildered after being betrayed by an affair since it is a form of betrayal. It is the pits. Couples who are dealing with infidelity are left to deal with the aftermath after they have processed the initial shock, disbelief, pain, and rage, as well as any other feelings that have been repressed or amplified. According to the findings of the research, there are three stages that need to be taken in order for a marriage to find healing after one of them has committed adultery. Couples can find healing from the wounds caused by infidelity by working through the three phases of affair discovery, which are atonement, attunement, and attachment.

1. Atonement

Atonement is not a word that is commonly used in everyday conversation, with the possible exception of when discussing religious topics. For the benefit of those who may have forgotten, atonement is defined as making amends for wrongdoing or injury. When viewed through the lens of an automobile crash, the explanation is quite straightforward. If someone is found to be at fault for an accident, the party found to be at fault (or, more accurately, the person's insurance company) is responsible for paying the injured party's medical bills as well as the amount of money required to repair or replace the damaged vehicle.

Atonement is far more difficult to achieve in a marriage that has already been broken up. After being in a car accident, most unfaithful partners probably have the same dream that they could just make a simple payment and put the whole thing behind them, just like you would do. But things don't really function like that in married relationships. Making amends requires patience, dedication, a willingness to risk being hurt, and most importantly, authenticity. The Atonement Stage allows room for the truth to emerge with the passage of time as well as for feelings of resentment, fear, guilt, and shame to diminish. The Atonement Phase has been described as "a tightrope that has to be walked very carefully, and with as much openness as possible." It is also essential to keep in mind that it is not uncommon for the truth to be revealed after some period of time has passed. There are a number of potential causes for this to occur. Frequently, the partner who is unfaithful has the mistaken belief that they are shielding either their partner or themselves from potential harm by withholding certain information. They might be concerned that it will be too much for them to deal with. They may still be grappling with feelings of attachment to their affair partner, which further complicates the situation when it comes to telling the truth. Because of this, it is common for the partner who is cheating to reveal new information after being prodded and during a variety of conversations. This is often difficult for the partner who has been betrayed.

2. Attunement

After the infidelity has been discovered, the couple will enter the Attunement Phase, during which they will be able to examine the aspects of their marriage that were problematic and may have had a role in the affair. It goes without saying that the partner who is cheating on their spouse is the one who is responsible for their conduct and cannot shift blame for the affair on the difficulties in the marriage. Despite this, they continued to make the regrettable decision to look outside of their marriage in order to fulfil their requirements. However, in order to progress, problems that have arisen in the marriage need to be resolved, and this task falls under the purview of the Attunement Phase. It can be useful for married couples to think of the time after an affair as the beginning of a new marriage, whether it be a second marriage or an improved marriage with the same partner. It is not productive to go back to the previous marriage in an effort to mend what was damaged in the relationship. It is more vital to be attentive to each other's needs and to develop a new relationship that is superior to the one that previously existed.

The process of continuing to heal from the trauma caused by the affair is another component of the Attunement Phase. Sincerity demands that I tell you that this process [of the betrayed working through their trauma] cannot take place soon enough for the betrayed, nor can it take place slowly enough for the betrayed. Post-infidelity stress disorder, often known as PISD, is a name that some psychologists use to describe what the partner who has been cheated on goes through. The betrayed partner frequently suffers symptoms that are very similar to those of PISD.

This is a severe form of relational trauma, and those of us who are familiar with PISD are aware that triggers can have a cumulative effect on people over time and even over the long term. If you are the partner that was cheated on and you are reading this, you should know that what you are going through is normal and it is alright. It is not a problem if getting through these stages takes a significant amount of time. And if you're the one who cheated on your partner, remember that you'll need to have compassion and understanding while they take the time they need to heal from the pain of your infidelity.

At the very least, in the beginning, it is typically recommended that the couple limit their discussion of the affair to their appointments with the counsellor. This will prevent the affair from becoming all-consuming and taking away from the spouse's family life, which is especially important in the event that the couple shares children. It is essential for kids to have some feeling of stability in their lives. And, if we're being completely honest, it's vital for the adults involved as well. If, on the other hand, you find that you simply cannot refrain from discussing the affair outside of therapy, you should establish a certain time to do so and restrict the total amount of time you spend doing so. Once more, this stops the scandal from becoming out of control and gaining even more influence than it already has.

3. Attachment

The true stage of reconciliation begins after an adulterous affair has been discovered and is known as the Attachment Stage. This is absolutely necessary in order to avoid having a marriage that is characterized by resentment, passive-aggressive conduct, and dissatisfaction. If, years after an affair, the betrayed spouse announces that they want a divorce because they never could get over the infidelity, this is a piece of strong evidence that the couple did not go through the Attachment Stage before ending their relationship. During the Attachment Stage, a couple will start to have a greater sense of sexual and physical connection with one another. It is essential that you reassure one another that you are still devoted to the endeavor and that you are still putting in the necessary effort. It is vitally crucial for the spouse who is working hard to repair trust in the relationship to have affirmation from the partner who has been harmed throughout the process. The path to a happy marriage does not include harboring resentment and mistrust for the rest of one's life. Keep in mind that this is your second marriage, and you want it to be even happier and more successful than the first one was.

In the Attachment Phase, the feelings of grief caused by the affair will continue to come and go in waves, as was indicated earlier. There is always the possibility that one partner will be the one to be triggered, and this has the potential to take feelings right back to that raw and authentic place they were in when the affair was initially discovered. During this stage, it is imperative that you are truthful with one another. Both honesty and consistent communication are necessary components of a good relationship. Instead of taking a defensive stance, try to put yourself in your partner's shoes and think about the things that trigger them and how they react to those things. Being defensive is a surefire way to get yourself into a downward emotional spiral, which is exactly the kind of place you do not want to be. In the event that the Attachment Stage is successful, the distance between triggers will gradually decrease. The level of pain decreases while simultaneously increasing trust and intimacy.

CHAPTERS 4
What to Do and What Not to Do After the Discovering an Affair

It is a difficult thing to go through a heartbreak and then make the conscious decision to go on with one's life. In spite of this, it is possible to have a more fulfilling marriage in the long run if both you and your partner have the correct frame of mind to progress and if you are both devoted to making this happen. Always be willing to tell the truth; more often than not, it is the lying that causes the most harm, not the sexual or emotional activity itself. The ability to heal and reestablish trust while also building hope for honesty in the future is fostered by the willingness to be honest.

Dos for The Strayed Partner

1. You must accept responsibility and answer for the harm that you have caused, both with your words and your deeds. Grab hold of it! Make it clear that you are willing to do whatever it takes to succeed. It can be difficult to resist the want to throw the finger at someone else, but this is not the time to criticize your partner.

2. Feel the anguish that you have caused other people and demonstrate that you are sorry.

3. Give your partner the opportunity to talk about what happened, ask questions, and discuss how they are feeling about it. Your partner is always going to be more interested in talking about it than you are going to be. Inquire with him or her about the factor that helps the greatest.

4. Have some patience. Betrayed people often find it difficult to move on with their lives. It is a significant loss, has the potential to flip your world upside down, and sends you on a roller coaster ride of emotions while your thoughts race at breakneck speed.

5. Give them complete access to all of your passwords, phones, and social media accounts, among other things.

6. Learn more about who you are. Find out why you were so miserable, what made you susceptible to having an affair, what worries and phobias you have, where you hid and did not face your unhappiness, and where you have the most room for personal development.

7. You should seek out individual as well as marriage counselling or spiritual direction to help you with your inner challenges and progress with your relationship issues and to analyze your childhood and the ways in

which it may have impacted your view of yourself and your expectations of marriage.

8. Be open and honest with your partner about what you are learning and recognizing your past mistakes, your strengths and shortcomings, your anxieties and insecurities, as well as your aspirations and desires.

9. You need to forgive yourself and get over your feelings of shame and guilt. Although it is essential that you feel the grief you have caused others, continuing to feel guilty about it and failing to forgive yourself will only prevent you and your partner from moving forward. It is healthy to express regret to your spouse, and you should continue to do so; nevertheless, you should be careful not to keep the second pang of guilt bottled up inside of you. It's okay; you screwed up—a huge one—but whatever happened in the past is already behind you. Now is the time to confront the future.

10. Acquire the skills necessary to love and accept yourself and take responsibility for your own happiness. Learn how you may have been giving away your power by looking for something or someone outside of yourself or your marriage to fill an emptiness. This emptiness could have been caused by a need for affirmation or admiration, a need for more attention to feel worthwhile,

or a dependency on feeling sexually desired. Develop the relationship with yourself, which is the most significant one you have. Doing so will place you in the best position possible to benefit to the greatest extent possible from the mended relationship.

What not to DO

1. Don't Place the Blame on Your Partner or on the Circumstances.
2. You shouldn't try to hide your regret or try to avoid the sorrow you're feeling.
3. You shouldn't avoid talking to people and listening to them.
4. Don't be in a hurry or put any pressure to move on.
5. Don't be dishonest when others ask you questions.
6. Protecting your electronic privacy is a bad idea.
7. Don't continue on the same path.
8. You shouldn't try to handle it on your own.
9. Don't let feelings of guilt and humiliation paralyze you.
10. Don't waste your time hunting for love in the wrong places.

DOs for The Betrayed Partner

1. Learn to ride out your own emotional storm and learn to quiet it. In the midst of the devastation and the roller coaster of insecurities and feelings, it is essential to be as proactive as possible in taking excellent care of yourself and to engage in that which calms you as much as possible. In addition, it is essential to be as proactive as possible in minimizing the negative effects of the situation. Now is the moment to build a safe haven for yourself by engaging in whatever routines you have found to help you feel more grounded, centered, and at peace. These routines can be done with or without your spouse. In the long run, regardless of what occurs around us or to us, our sense of agency and happiness will increase proportionately to the degree to which we accept responsibility for our feelings and our lives. Help someone else out by rendering service. Even if it's only for five minutes every single day. The finest method to help yourself and get in touch with your true self is to assist another person in need. Having this knowledge will assist you in gaining clarity during the process.

2. Acquire an understanding of your cheating partner. Many people get immediately fascinated with wanting to know WHY and HOW COULD S/HE (for which it is

frequently impossible to comprehend or be satisfied by a sensible explanation), and this obsession takes over their lives almost immediately. In spite of the fact that this type of compulsive thinking can be detrimental, it can be therapeutic to start the process of knowing your spouse in order to begin the healing process. You will be able to remove yourself from the situation and gain some perspective and detachment the sooner you are able to have empathy and comprehend what your partner is struggling with or what they need to overcome. The more we are able to fight off the temptation to adopt a victim mentality, the sooner we will be able to emerge from the shadows and start the process of getting better.

3. Strive toward greater self-awareness and personal development. Our bodies are designed to have blind spots. We are here to take part in a process that will remove the obstacles that prevent us from experiencing genuine love. Even though you are not accountable for the activities of your husband or mate, the quicker we can open ourselves to what this suffering is here to teach us, the quicker the healing process speeds in quantum proportion. This is true even though you are not responsible for the conduct of your partner. It is essential to have a solid understanding of your attachment issues, as well as your insecurities and

worries, as well as how these things manifest themselves in your life and relationship and cause you problems. Knowledge is the bridge that allows us to connect to our true selves, and the bridge that we build to our true selves is the most essential relationship in our lives.

4. Determine the best course of action. In most cases, it is advisable to wait before making a decision and not to act rashly. When one is just beginning the process of healing, it is difficult to anticipate how feelings might change and how the dynamics can transform throughout the course of the process. Because there are many different kinds of affairs, individual differences in how each person reacts to betrayal, different upbringings and ideals around marriage, and the foundation of the relationship at the time of the affair, it is difficult to give an accurate estimate regarding the percentage of marriages that are able to recover. Having said that, a greater percentage of relationships succeed than fail, and a good number of them improve over time. There are a lot of different aspects at play, and there are some very crucial questions that one should ask themselves.

5. Learn to forgive yourself first, and then learn to forgive your partner if they've been unfaithful. We are given the opportunity to fall short, gain wisdom from our

experiences, and progress as a result. The mentality that we are never really victims is another thing that works to our advantage. When we look at everything that occurs in our lives as a potential learning experience, we are given the gift of living as an empowered and creative soul rather than being at the impact of being at the mercy of our surroundings. The act of forgiving another person is not a simple undertaking; yet, once the burden of blame is lifted from our shoulders, the gravity of many other painful feelings also begins to dissipate.

What not to DO

1. Don't let your feelings of victimization consume you to the point of obsession.

2. Don't try to get away from your suffering.

3. You shouldn't be the one to blame. This is not the same as taking responsibility for something.

4. Believing that you are too weak to ask for assistance is a common misconception, especially when a recent betrayal has reopened old wounds.

5. Don't bottle up how you're feeling; express them.

6. Do not ignore the void that exists within you just because it is too painful or you feel like you are too weak to deal with it.

7. Be careful not to vent your frustrations to the wrong individuals. It is in your best interest to avoid seeking out people who continually agree with you and who fuel your anger by encouraging you to take action.

8. Don't Idealize the past. Obsessing over the good times that are gone.

9. When the voice of your ego tells you that you are unworthy, you shouldn't believe it.

CHAPTERS 5
Reestablishing Sexual Intimacy

It is common for the encounter to be passionate and emotionally fraught when a person returns to sexual intimacy after having an affair. After an affair has been revealed, just the thought of resuming sexual activity can cause both partners to feel a range of emotions, including anticipation and longing, worry and anxiety, and even dread in some cases.

There isn't just one "correct" approach to restarting sexual intimacy after one partner has had an affair; rather, there are a few different blunders that can be made along the route by couples. Because you don't always know what the triggers and reminders are until you encounter them; unfortunately, the majority of you won't be able to process or heal everything before interacting sexually. This will be the case because you can't always predict what they will be. Therefore, it is essential to move cautiously through this stage. When one spouse has wandered away from the relationship, the other may try to force sex as a method to prove to the other that they still love and desire them. They may be feeling so much guilt and shame that they are unable to have sex with the other person because they want to show them that they want to be with them. They could be worried about aggravating their partner's wounds or bringing up painful memories of the affair. On the other hand, the spouse who was betrayed may either be too upset or furious to experience sexual attraction or may wish to use sex as a means to prove their worth to their partner, stay on to the relationship, and push the affair partner out of his or her mind. It is essential to avoid jumping into physical intimacy too quickly or relying on sexual activity to keep the relationship together. From what I've seen, the primary focus should be on rebuilding the emotional connection and trust that formerly existed. When you and your partner have reached a point where you feel emotionally close to one another, sexual closeness will return naturally. But returning to sexual activity when there is a lack of trust and closeness between the partners is a recipe for disaster. "Sex does not lead to emotional intimacy; however, emotional intimacy can lead to physical intimacy." Here are some suggestions that will help you on your journey to reestablishing sexual intimacy with your spouse and your own sexual wholeness.

1. It is a deeply personal decision whether and how to restart sexual intimacy following an affair, and neither

partner should ever feel compelled to do so before they are confident that they are emotionally, mentally, and physically prepared to do so. It is recommended that couples refrain from having sexual activity for at least three months in order to rebuild their emotional connection before engaging in sexual activity again.

2. One of the most important things for partners to experience after learning that their partner has had an affair or is addicted to sexual activity is empathy. It should come as no surprise that the unfaithful partner also has a need for empathy and compassion, but the fact that they do is likely to come as a surprise to the partner who was unfaithful. However, both spouses are probably going through an emotional roller coaster, and they both require the acknowledgement of what they are going through from their partners.

3. The mind is sometimes one of the most significant barriers to resuming physical closeness, particularly for the partner who has been betrayed. In the first phases of restarting sexual activity, one may find that memories and pictures, whether they are genuine or imagined, might intrude on and disrupt the experience. It could be beneficial to maintain a connection by keeping your eyes open and looking at one other when you are engaging in

sexual activity together. When you look into the eyes of your partner, it not only lets you know that they are present in the moment with you, but it also helps you stay present in the moment with them. If you are still having trouble with images and videos playing in your head during sex, one more useful strategy is to agree to stop what you are doing and name what is going on in your thoughts. This can help you overcome this issue. This gives your partner the opportunity to listen as well as demonstrate empathy, compassion, and care for you. It's not uncommon to be able to pick up just where you left off after only a few minutes' break. It is not a good idea to try to force your way through those disruptive thoughts. You will only make the situation worse.

4. Resentments are likely one of the most significant obstacles in the way of reigniting desire. If you find that this is a problem for you, you will need to devise a strategy to overcome these challenges. Examine the opportunity cost of why you are keeping hold of them. What are the advantages of harboring ill will against others? Do you feel empowered or as if you have the upper hand when you're among them? Or do you avoid confrontation out of fear? Be conscious of the fact that resentment can manifest in a variety of ways, including

but not limited to wrath, bitterness, withdrawal, melancholy, and impatience. There are other costs to one's body, such as increased risk of cardiovascular disease, high blood pressure, stroke, and a weakened immune system. If you battle with any of those physical symptoms, I am not suggesting that resentments are the source of those symptoms, but they can contribute to those symptoms.

5. Both partners need to get tested for sexually transmitted infections (STIs), and if necessary, you should talk to a therapist about how to process your reaction.

6. Pay attention to how your body reacts to feelings of shame, fear, anxiety, and stress, as well as how the body of your partner reacts. At this point, the body may have a numbing sensation, and the senses may feel muted. This is typically a symptom of trauma, either trauma caused by the betrayal or trauma from the past that is being reactivated as a result of the betrayal.

7. Both partners should be prepared to have healthy dialogues and maybe make accommodations to the requirements of the other. Sexual difficulties, such as a lack of desire, arousal, or capacity to climax, should be verbally addressed, and both couples should acknowledge that they are prepared to have those conversations.

CHAPTER 6
Moving On, Going Separate Ways

When you notice that love is beginning to hurt you, it is probably time to take a step back and examine the circumstances around your relationship. There is no such thing as a perfect romantic relationship, and unfortunately, pain is an inevitability in almost all of them. On the other hand, there are circumstances in which the pain caused by your relationship may be sufficient to motivate you to take action. You are the only person who can determine how far you are willing to go with this situation: whether to continue working on the relationship, wait for things to change, or end it.

If you are still feeling overly impacted and upset by everything that took place, it is not the best time to make significant decisions. The vast majority of people have a propensity to make this error, which frequently leads to more terrible and equally painful repercussions later on. It can be reassuring to assume that your first response; like leaving, going away, or even burning bridges, is an indication that you can easily move on, but in reality, you are only making things more difficult for yourself.

The Post-Broken-Up-Relationship Syndrome

How can you tell if you are going through the regular stages of getting over a break-up or if you are experiencing something more extreme? To put it simply, you will feel all of the following at some point or another:

• During the first one to two weeks, you won't be able to sleep or eat normally.

• Either you lose weight, or you gain weight.

• You look at your phone every five minutes in the hopes that your former partner has given you a message.

• You are pondering your actions and wondering where you went wrong.

• You believe that if you had been more attractive to your ex, he or she would not have been able to leave you.

• Your thoughts are debating whether or not you should delete all of your photos together.

• You find yourself thinking about your ex in every nook and cranny of your home, your neighborhood, and pretty much everywhere else.

Do not be afraid of what you are going through because these are all typical responses that a normal person would have in the midst of tragedy. They will end in a short while.

In the event that the relationship has come to an end, the following activities are included in the process of self-recovery:

1. Allow yourself the time and space you need to remain calm.

Allowing oneself the time and space to calm down after a break-up is an important step in the process of dealing with the emotional fallout of a relationship ending. To begin, you need to acquire the skills necessary to rid yourself of all the unfavorable and pointless emotional baggage that you have been unable to let go of in the past. You should make an effort to let go of these poisonous sentiments before it is too late. Examples of these unhealthy emotions that can triple the weight of the emotional burden include anger and bitterness. Try to let go of these feelings before it is too late.

2. Reassure yourself that it is acceptable to not be completely okay.

Some people who are going through the emotional and psychological fallout of a break-up have the misconception that being strong involves denying the fact that they are not doing okay after the break-up. This attitude of denial that they are unaffected and that they should not feel wounded might be harmful rather than helpful in the long run. The suppression of these feelings may have long-term ramifications, and it's only a matter of time before they come bursting out of you. Reassure yourself that it is fine to feel whatever it is that you are feeling right now. Tell yourself that it is acceptable to cry, that it is normal to be vulnerable, and that it is okay to confess that you are weak. It's an essential step in the procedure.

3. Learn how to love yourself and put that love into practice without feeling guilty about it.
Changing things up in life, such as going on adventures, discovering new things, or starting fresh with new hobbies and pursuits. Doing the things that you were restricted from doing while you were in a relationship with someone else. You should have love for yourself, and you should never, under any circumstances, allow anyone to accuse you of being selfish simply because you opted to put yourself first. An emotionally taxing experience might result from the end of a destructive relationship. It is especially true if you have invested everything and every part of yourself in that relationship,

only to find out that you have lost yourself in the process of doing so. Because this tiredness might make you feel less confident, uninspired, bored, and even unwilling to try new things, it is crucial to know where you can get that emotional refill and confidence boost in order to combat these feelings. Restore your confidence and self-esteem. Instead of dwelling on the attributes that you lack, put your attention on the positive aspects of who you are and the contributions that you made to the relationship.

4. Concentrate on the positive aspects of yourself.

Put it in writing, either using a pen and paper or the Notes app on your phone, so that you may see it every day and be reminded of how deserving you are of being loved. Make a list and think of qualities that speak to your character, emotional strengths, skill sets, abilities, and anything else that has value in a relationship. These can be written down and thought of as you make the list. If you are having trouble coming up with ideas, talk to your closest friends and family members. They will be thrilled to have the opportunity to tell you all the ways in which they consider themselves fortunate to have you in their lives.

5. Put in place the appropriate network of support for yourself.

Spending quality time with close friends who you might not have seen as much while you were in a relationship is the ideal opportunity that presents itself immediately after a split. You won't have to worry about feeling lonely thanks to their presence. When going through the most difficult parts of a break-up, it is extremely crucial to have a strong support system of individuals you know you can trust. Hang out with friends who are willing to hear your tale, and spend time with folks who sincerely want the best for you. Keep in mind that while some people may want to comfort you after the split, others may try to bring you back to the harsh truth that you must now confront. Some kinds of guidance might be encouraging, while other pieces of guidance can be direct and can make the hurt feel much worse. Take what you can from each of them, but ultimately you are responsible for your own actions and choices.

6. It's best not to chase after rebounds.

There's a good reason why they're such a cliché: rebounds provide a rapid boost that, for the time being at least, will make you feel sexy or worthwhile. But once the high has worn off, you might merely feel bad about what you did. If you are attempting to find a way to avoid feeling the unpleasant feelings that come with losing someone you loved, then making hasty judgments is a sign that you are trying to find a way to avoid feeling those emotions. Recognize the pain you are experiencing and accept the fact that being a responsible person requires you to address it.

7. Let go of the concept that there will ever be "closure."

Even while we all know that real life doesn't go the way a romantic comedy does, you could find yourself wishing you had a dramatic break-up anyhow, even if it didn't happen to you. Sadly, what tends to occur more frequently is that two individuals steadily drift apart from one another, and after the break-up, one of you is left asking, why? It is healthier (and better for your long-term mental health) to recognize and accept that you just weren't the right match for each other. Instead of beating yourself up looking for explanations, it is better for your long-term mental health to know and accept this. If the other person is unable to explain why they no longer want to be with you, you should convince yourself that the fact that your ex-partner was unable to make the relationship work for its whole duration is all the justification you require to properly close that chapter of your life. The underlying meanings of such explanations are as follows: "I deserve someone who is capable of making a commitment," "I deserve someone who can love me enough," and "I deserve someone who appreciates everything about me."

8. Seek out social support and introduce yourself to new people.

Finding social support, creating new acquaintances, and meeting new people will provide you the opportunity to forget about your previous partner and go on to a better person in your life. Participating in social activities can assist you in regaining your self-assurance. I'm not suggesting that you go looking for a new partner. Make sure that you have completely let go of the past before you start dating someone fresh so that you won't bring any baggage into the relationship. Having a large number of friends, on the other hand, is not necessarily a negative thing.

9. Maintain a focus on your career.

Being single provides you with the freedom to concentrate on achieving your goals and advancing your career. When you and your children are starving in the future, love won't be enough to keep you alive on its own. Therefore, make it a goal to become an independent person with a secure career. This can help you strengthen your sense of self-worth, and even if you suffer another heartbreak, it will still be there even after that. After a break-up, keeping yourself busy with work can help prevent you from dwelling on the relationship that once was. Unbeknownst to you, several months have already passed, and now you realize that you've moved on to other things. When you've been through a lot of unpleasant feelings, having successes in your professional life might provide you more reasons to look at life in a more optimistic light. This is especially true after you've experienced those negative feelings.

10. Try moving to a different location.

Do this only if, months after the break-up, you still find that you are unable to function regularly and that your depression is too severe. Moving to a new location is not such a bad idea if your present place of employment or neighborhood frequently brings up negative memories of your previous relationship, particularly if your ex-partner lives in the immediate area. You have the option to relocate to a different setting and start over. A new beginning gives you the opportunity to start over and find your bearings.

IN SUMMARY TERMS

There are a lot of different reasons why someone might cheat on their partner, but the fact that cheating hurts both parties is indisputable, and as a result, none of those justifications are really acceptable. The feelings that arise as a result of cheating can be intense and overpowering at times. Someone's sense of self-worth can be completely destroyed by being cheated on, which can leave them feeling sad and even hopeless as if they are unworthy of ever receiving love again. This hurt is made much worse by the fact that cheating typically takes place in the context of relationships, which is precisely the kind of setting in which trust is crucial. Consider the following: you have placed all of your faith in another individual, entrusting them with the responsibility of guiding your life into the future, only for them to blow it all. Even worse, they did not have the maturity to tell you directly before they left you for someone else.

When there is a breach of trust in a relationship, it can be challenging to reestablish that relationship. It's a living hell. The most effective method for recovering emotionally from a traumatic love experience is to turn inward and, with the help of writing and meditation, locate the origin of one's fears.